I Loved You with a Truly Unique and Genuine Love

Kyu? Hai na special?, Volume 3

Mrigendra Bharti

Published by Sellbrochure Vymish Entertainment, 2024.

I LOVED YOU WITH A TRULY UNIQUE AND GENUINE LOVE

First edition. September 12, 2024.

Copyright © 2024 Mrigendra Bharti.

ISBN: 979-8227192332

Written by Mrigendra Bharti.

Table of Contents

For Her

To My Princess,

This book stands as a testament to you, a canvas where every word and every poem is imbued with the hues of my deepest affection. As you turn these pages, know that each line reflects how uniquely you inspire me. This collection is more than just poetry—it is my heartfelt declaration that you are unlike anyone else in my life.

In a world overflowing with ordinary expressions, I sought to offer you something truly extraordinary. I wanted to create a tribute as distinctive and beautiful as you are. Each poem is a whisper of my admiration, a celebration of the way you illuminate my world. Your presence is a rare and wonderful gift, and I aimed to capture that exceptional quality in these verses.

Your smile, your laughter, and the way you brighten even the dullest of days are the true muses behind this book. This journey through my feelings is expressed in ways I hope will make your heart flutter and your cheeks blush. You deserve a love as special as you are, and this collection is my attempt to offer just that.

As you read these poems, remember they are crafted with you in mind. They represent my deep appreciation and the profound impact you have on my life. This book is for you and you alone—my muse, my inspiration, my everything.

With all my love,
Mrigendra Bharti

Preface

In the quiet moments of reflection and the gentle whispers of my heart, I have come to realize that words alone cannot fully capture the depth of my feelings for you. Yet, in these pages, I have endeavored to do just that. "I Loved You with a Truly Unique and Genuine Love" is more than a collection of poems—it is a heartfelt testament to a love that stands apart, a love that I believe is truly unparalleled.

Every poem within this book is crafted with the utmost care, inspired by the extraordinary way you illuminate my world. Your presence brings a warmth and a light that are beyond compare, and these verses are a celebration of that exceptional quality. Each line is a reflection of how deeply you inspire me, how profoundly you touch my life.

In a world full of ordinary expressions, I wanted to give you something that mirrors the uniqueness of our bond. These poems are my way of saying that you are not just another person in my life; you are a rare and cherished presence, deserving of a love that is as special and exceptional as you are.

Your smile, your laughter, and the way you make even the dullest moments shine brightly are the true muses behind this book. It is my hope that as you read through these poems, you will feel the depth of my affection and the sincerity of my emotions. This book is a tribute to you and to the love we share—a love that is truly one of a kind.

Thank you for being the inspiration behind these verses, and for filling my life with a love that is as unique and genuine as you are. With all my love,
Mrigendra Bharti

Series Overview: Kyu? Hai na Special?

In a world where expressions of love often blend into the mundane, Kyu? Hai na Special? stands as a beacon of originality. This series, crafted with deep admiration and affection, explores a distinctive approach to celebrating someone truly exceptional. The title itself poses a question that invites curiosity—why is this approach special? The answer lies in the way each book is meticulously designed to honor a singular muse, whose essence and charm transcend the ordinary. Every poem and every word within these pages are dedicated to a princess-like figure, embodying grace and elegance that inspire each verse.

As you journey through this series, you will discover that each book is not just a collection of poems but a tribute to a unique individual whose impact is both profound and unparalleled. The distinctive approach captured in these works reflects a heartfelt dedication, celebrating a presence that turns the everyday into something extraordinary.

Kyu? Hai na Special? is more than just a title—it is a declaration of the exceptional nature of the muse behind these verses and an invitation to experience love expressed in a truly remarkable way.

Acknowledgment

In the quiet moments of reflection, I find myself overwhelmed with gratitude for the inspiration behind this book. This collection of poems is dedicated to a remarkable presence, a person whose essence has infused every word and sentiment within these pages.

To the one whose grace and charm have transformed the ordinary into the extraordinary, I extend my deepest thanks. Your influence has shaped these verses and turned them into a celebration of the unique and the beautiful. It is your spirit that has guided each line, and your elegance that has inspired each thought.

Though your name remains unspoken, your impact is profoundly felt in every stanza. This book stands as a testament to the admiration and affection you have sparked. Your presence has been the muse that turned fleeting moments into lasting expressions of love.

Thank you for being a beacon of inspiration. This work is a tribute to you and a reflection of the exceptional qualities that make you truly special.

With heartfelt appreciation,
Mrigendra Bharti

About Sellbrochure IPDP

Sellbrochure Vymish Entertainment, recognized as India's largest book publishing company, has made significant strides in ensuring its extensive collection of books reaches audiences across the global market. This rapid expansion is a testament to the company's dedication to disseminating knowledge and literature far beyond national borders. Central to its success is its affiliation with InkWhirl Media Networks, a reputable entity in the media and publication industry known for its innovative and strategic approaches. Within this network, InkWhirl Publication LLC operates as a vital division, further enhancing the company's capabilities and reach in the international market. The visionary behind this enterprise is Mrigendra Bharti, the founder of Sellbrochure Vymish Entertainment. His foresight and passion for the literary world have been instrumental in steering the company towards remarkable growth and recognition. Under his leadership, Sellbrochure Vymish Entertainment has not only expanded its catalog but also established a strong presence in both domestic and international markets. Mrigendra Bharti's commitment to excellence and innovation has been a driving force in the company's journey, ensuring that it stays ahead of industry trends and meets the evolving needs of readers worldwide.

Sellbrochure Vymish Entertainment operates under the robust support of its parental organization, Mrigendra Bharti Group InfoTech. This affiliation provides the necessary resources and strategic guidance, enabling the publishing company to undertake ambitious projects and explore new markets. Mrigendra Bharti Group InfoTech's extensive experience in technology and information services has been a valuable asset, allowing Sellbrochure Vymish Entertainment to integrate advanced digital solutions in its operations, thereby enhancing its distribution capabilities and reader engagement.

Through relentless efforts and a commitment to quality, Sellbrochure Vymish Entertainment continues to break barriers and expand the reach of Indian literature globally. The company's diverse portfolio includes a wide range of genres, catering to different age groups and interests, thereby fostering a rich and inclusive reading culture. As it continues to innovate and grow, Sellbrochure Vymish Entertainment remains dedicated to its mission of making literature accessible to all, contributing significantly to the global literary landscape.

Connect With Mrigendra,

Thank you very much for choosing this book.

You can also connect with me on Instagram,

https://www.instagram.com/i_mrigendrabharti.official

With Love,

Mrigendra Bharti

Introduction

Welcome to "I Loved You with a Truly Unique and Genuine Love," a collection of poems born from the deepest corners of my heart. This book is a tribute to a love that transcends the ordinary, a love that is as exceptional and unparalleled as you are to me.

In these pages, you will find a series of verses that capture the essence of my feelings—a love that is both profound and extraordinary. Each poem is a reflection of how you inspire me, how you bring light and joy into my life in ways that words alone cannot fully express.

This collection is not just an anthology of poetry but a personal journey through the emotions and experiences that define my love for you. It's my attempt to convey, through carefully chosen words and heartfelt sentiments, just how uniquely special our bond is.

The poems in this book are meant to celebrate you—your presence, your smile, your laughter, and the countless ways you brighten my days. They are crafted to honor a love that stands apart, to show that you are not just another person in my life, but a rare and cherished treasure.

As you read through these pages, I hope you feel the depth of my affection and the sincerity behind each line. This book is a reflection of my heartfelt gratitude for having you in my life, and a testament to a love that is truly one of a kind.

Thank you for being the muse and inspiration behind this collection. Your presence in my life has made it richer and more beautiful, and this book is a small token of the immense love and appreciation I hold for you.

So let's start.......

Endless Echoes of You

In the quiet whispers of the dawn,
Your name is carved where light is drawn,
Each breath of mine, a silent vow,
I loved you then, I love you now.
The world may change, the seasons turn,
But in my soul, your fire will burn.
Not fleeting like the autumn's wind,
But endless, like the skies that bend.
A love so deep, untouched by time,
Beyond the stars, beyond the rhyme.
No words could ever quite convey,
The way I love you, night and day.

The Unwritten Story

In every glance, in every sigh,
You are the ink beneath my sky.
Each chapter, page, and word is new,
Because my story is only you.
Your eyes, the stars I navigate,
Through every storm, through every fate.
A love so pure, so deeply true,
No other soul could ever do.
And if this world could fade away,
I'd still have you, come what may.
For even time cannot erase,
The sacred love in your embrace.

Beyond Every Horizon

I sought no end, I sought no start,
I found it all within your heart.
A love that blooms beyond the day,
A love that will not fade away.
Through darkest nights, through brightest dawns,
You are the wind that always spawns
A hope that lingers in the air,
A love so honest, rare, and fair.
No sky too high, no sea too deep,
Your love is all I wish to keep.
In every beat, in every breath,
It's you I'll love beyond all death.

A Love Like Mine

I've known no love like this before,
A love that leaves me wanting more.
Not bound by fear or fleeting flame,
But burning wild, without a name.
A love so vast, it breaks the sky,
A love where even tears won't lie.
For every moment shared with you,
Is proof that dreams can still come true.
No boundaries hold, no walls confine,
This love, my dear, is truly mine.
And in your arms, I've found my place,
An endless warmth, a sweet embrace.

Whispers in the Wind

The wind it carries words of grace,
Each whisper wrapped in your embrace.
I close my eyes and feel you near,
Your voice, your touch, forever here.
In every step, in every mile,
I've loved you all the while.
A love so real, so deeply pure,
With you, my heart will always endure.
And though the world may never see,
How much you mean, how much to me,
I'll write my love across the stars,
And keep you close, no matter how far.

More Than Just Forever

If forever was a moment's span,
I'd stretch it farther than life began.
For in your eyes, I found the truth,
That love like ours defies all proof.
Not just a word, not just a phrase,
But a feeling that sets my soul ablaze.
It's in the way you breathe my name,
A love untouched, unscarred by flame.
I've wandered worlds just to see,
That no one loves as much as me.
For mine is endless, pure, and wide,
Like oceans pulled by moonlit tides.
More than just forever, it seems,
You are the source of all my dreams.
A love so deep, no words could say,
How I adore you, every day.

Boundless

I've tied no strings, yet we are bound,
In ways that words may not be found.
A love so fierce, so raw, so true,
That only hearts like mine and you
Could understand the sacred art,
Of loving with an open heart.
The stars, they envy what we share,
For even they could not compare.
Your touch, your smile, your very soul,
Have made me feel entirely whole.
And though the world may doubt this fire,
It fuels my every breath, desire.
For none have loved the way I do,
And none will ever rival you.

A Love Unwritten

If poets spoke of love untold,
They'd weave us into lines of gold.
For no one sees, and no one knows,
The way my love for you still grows.
It's not in grand or fleeting shows,
But in the quiet, where it glows.
In every glance, in every pause,
It lives without the need for cause.
The world can spin, the rivers bend,
But my love, my dear, will never end.
For though no script can capture this,
Our love is carved in endless bliss.
Unwritten, boundless, pure as light,
I'll hold you close, through every fight.
For even silence speaks so loud,
When love like ours wears heaven's shroud.

The Depth You'll Never See

I've loved you in the spaces vast,
Where time dissolves, where moments pass.
In every breath, in every tear,
I've held you close, I've kept you near.
No one could love the way I do,
For none could feel this deep, this true.
It's in the way the world stands still,
When I think of you, against my will.
You'll never know the depth I hide,
The way I ache to stay beside.
But even if the earth should break,
It's only you my heart will take.
For love like ours is hard to find,
A bond that stretches through the mind.
And though the world may never see,
I'll love you deeper, endlessly.

In the Silence, I'm Yours

In the silence where others fade,
My love for you will never jade.
In moments when the world seems still,
I love you more against my will.
Not bound by time, not chained by fate,
A love so deep, it resonates.
It hums in every quiet breath,
It lingers on, defying death.
They say true love is hard to find,
But in you, darling, I've entwined
A part of me no one can claim,
A love too deep, too wild to tame.
So when the world grows cold and dark,
Just know you carry all my spark.
For in the silence, I am yours,
A love that echoes and endures.

This Love, Unmatched

I've walked the roads where hearts have bled,
But none have felt what ours has said.
For love like this is rare and bright,
A beacon in the endless night.
No song could ever play our tune,
For we have danced beneath the moon
In ways that leave the stars in awe,
A love without a single flaw.
I see it when you look at me,
A kind of love that sets me free.
And though the world will never know,
I'll love you more than I could show.
For love like ours, it bends, it grows,
Unmatched by all the highs and lows.
And if the world should fall apart,
I'll still hold you within my heart.

The Only Love I Know

I've tried to find the words to say,
How much you mean to me each day.
But nothing comes, for love like this,
Is more than just a fleeting kiss.
It's in the way you fill my soul,
The way you make me feel so whole.
No one has loved the way I do,
No one could ever match my view.
For you, my dear, are more than life,
The reason I can bear the strife.
And though the world may never see,
It's only you who completes me.
So when they ask if love is real,
I'll tell them what I truly feel—
That you, my love, are all I know,
The only heart I'll ever show.

Beyond What Eyes Can See

Your name is carved upon my heart,
A mark so deep, it can't depart.
They say love's found in what we view,
But what I feel goes far past you.
It's in the spaces none can see,
In hidden realms of you and me.
A bond that stretches, never ends,
A love that even time defends.
You are the pulse within my soul,
The piece that makes me truly whole.
And though the world may not believe,
In you, my love, I can't deceive.
For what we have, no one could find,
A love so rare, so pure, so kind.
Beyond what eyes can hope to see,
I love you for eternity.

Untouched by Time

A thousand lifetimes could unfold,
But still, our love would not grow old.
It's written in the winds and skies,
A love that never fades or dies.
While others come and others go,
Our bond, my dear, will always grow.
For what we share is more than real,
A love no other heart could steal.
The stars above, they envy this,
For in your touch, I find my bliss.
A love untouched by fleeting years,
A love that melts away all fears.
So let the hours pass us by,
And let the sun fall from the sky.
For even time can't take away,
The way I love you more each day.

The Heart's Secret Language

No words can speak the way I feel,
For love like ours is too surreal.
It's not in phrases or in sound,
But in the way our souls are bound.
A quiet glance, a simple touch,
Says more than language ever could.
The world may try, but they won't know,
How deep this love of ours will grow.
In every silence, we remain,
A love that's free from doubt or pain.
It whispers softly in the night,
It shines beyond the brightest light.
So let them wonder, let them guess,
But they'll never truly witness
The secret way my heart still sings,
The joy your love forever brings.

A Fire That Never Fades

Some loves are soft, like autumn leaves,
But ours burns bright, it never grieves.
A flame that dances in the night,
A fire that fills my soul with light.
In every moment, every thought,
It's you I've loved, it's you I've sought.
No one could ever match this fire,
No heart could ever reach this higher.
You are the warmth inside my veins,
The only one who breaks my chains.
For even when the embers die,
You set the stars within my sky.
A love that never fades away,
A fire that burns through every day.
And in your arms, I'm truly free,
For you're the only flame for me.

The Love That Breaks All Boundaries

I've crossed the seas, I've climbed the skies,
But nothing compares to your eyes.
For in them lies a world so vast,
A love that's built to always last.
No wall can hold, no chain can bind,
The love that's carved within my mind.
It breaks the rules, defies the law,
For you, my dear, are my last straw.
I love you past what words can say,
I love you in the quiet way
That goes beyond what's seen or heard,
A love that needs no spoken word.
So let the boundaries fall apart,
For you've already won my heart.
And in this love, we'll always stay,
Unbound, unfazed, come what may.

Written in the Stars

The stars above, they write our tale,
A love that none could ever fail.
Each twinkling light, a secret shared,
A love that's bold, a love that's dared.
For even stars cannot compare,
To what we've built, to how we care.
A love so strong, so deep, so true,
That nothing else could see us through.
The galaxies, they hold our name,
A love untouched by doubt or shame.
For we were written in the skies,
A love that never truly dies.
So let the stars keep shining bright,
For you're my day, and you're my night.
And every wish they hold above,
Is nothing next to our great love.

This Love Will Never End

They'll tell you love is fleeting, brief,
A moment's joy, a flash of grief.
But what I feel, it's here to stay,
A love that will not fade away.
Through every storm, through every tide,
I've loved you deeply, far and wide.
No force could ever make me bend,
For this is love that will not end.
And even if the world should fall,
I'd still be here, I'd give my all.
For love like this is rare and strong,
It writes the words to every song.
So take my hand, and don't let go,
For what we have, the world won't know.
But I will love you 'til the end,
My lover, my heart, my closest friend.

In Every Breath, It's You

In every breath, it's you I feel,
A love so vast, so bright, so real.
It lingers in the quiet air,
A love no other could compare.
No need for grand or mighty shows,
For in my heart, your presence grows.
And though the world may never see,
It's only you who sets me free.
You are the rhythm in my chest,
The one who makes me feel my best.
And even in the darkest hours,
Your love blooms like the rarest flowers.
So when the world fades into night,
Just know with you, I've found my light.
For in each breath, in every view,
It's you I love, it's always you.

Deeper Than the Ocean's Depth

The ocean holds its secrets deep,
But not as deep as love we keep.
Beneath the waves, beyond the shore,
Is love like ours, forevermore.
The tides may rise, the winds may blow,
But still, my love for you will grow.
No depth could ever hide this fire,
No wave could quench this pure desire.
For in your eyes, I lose my way,
Yet find my home, where I shall stay.
A love so vast, it can't be found,
It's deeper still, it knows no bound.
So let the ocean take its toll,
For you, my love, complete my soul.
And in this sea, I'll gladly drown,
For you're the one I've always found.

Whispered in the Winds

The winds may carry many tales,
Of ships that crash and lovers' fails.
But in the breeze, I hear your name,
A love so bright, it can't be tamed.
It whispers gently in my ear,
And wipes away each doubt, each fear.
For even if the world grows cold,
This love of ours will still be bold.
Through every storm, through every gust,
I know in you, I place my trust.
No force could tear us both apart,
For you, my dear, you own my heart.
So let the winds blow where they may,
I'll love you more with each new day.
And though they howl, though they may bend,
Our love is one that will not end.

In the Space Between Our Words

In the quiet moments, in the hush,
That's where I find my greatest rush.
It's in the space between each sound,
Where love, so pure, is tightly bound.
We don't need words to feel this way,
For in your silence, I will stay.
A glance, a touch, a simple smile,
Makes every moment worth the while.
No one could ever understand,
The love we hold, the life we've planned.
For even when the words are few,
I still know all my heart wants: you.
And though the world may never see,
The depth of love 'tween you and me,
I cherish every quiet scene,
For that's where love is truly seen.

A Love That Needs No Reason

Some ask for reasons to explain,
But love like ours defies the brain.
I cannot tell you how or why,
I just know, love, I'd rather die—
Than live a life without your grace,
Without your warmth, without your face.
For love like this can't be explained,
It's not a rule that can be tamed.
It doesn't follow paths or signs,
It doesn't wait for perfect lines.
It simply grows, it simply lives,
And all it does is truly give.
So when they ask me why it's true,
I'll simply smile, and say, "It's you."
For love like ours needs no real reason,
It blooms through every time and season.

Through Every Lifetime

If I could live a thousand lives,
In every one, you'd still survive.
For even if the faces change,
My love for you would not rearrange.
In every time, in every space,
I'd find you still, I'd know your face.
For love like this, it knows no end,
It's you, my dear, my soul's best friend.
And though the world may twist and turn,
Our love will always brightly burn.
For even death could not erase,
The way I feel, the way you grace—
My life, my heart, my every thought,
For love like ours can't be forgot.
So through each life, I'll seek you out,
And love you still, without a doubt.

In Your Arms, I Am Free

Some search for freedom far and wide,
But in your arms, it's where I hide.
For there, I'm free from every care,
A love so pure, so true, so rare.
You hold me close, and in your touch,
I find my strength, my peace, my much.
The world outside may rage and tear,
But I have all I need in there.
Your love, it frees me from the chains,
It wipes away my past, my pains.
For in your arms, I find my flight,
A love that soars through darkest night.
So let them search, let them not see,
For only you can make me free.
And in your hold, I will remain,
A love that nothing could contain.

A Love the Sun Envy's

The sun above can light the sky,
But it can't love the way I try.
For even in its brightest flame,
It cannot match the way I name—
Your heart, your soul, the way you move,
The way your love has made me prove
That light exists beyond the stars,
In every moment that is ours.
The sun may rise, it may go down,
But in your love, I never frown.
For you are brighter still than this,
A love that none could dare dismiss.
So let the sun watch from above,
It cannot touch the way I love.
For even in its warmest rays,
It can't outshine my endless praise.

A Dream That Won't Depart

You are the dream I always keep,
A love that never falls asleep.
Though others fade when night is done,
In you, my love, I've just begun.
For even when the morning breaks,
It's you, my dear, that my heart takes.
No dream could ever match the feel,
Of knowing that this love is real.
You are the wish I hold so dear,
The one that brings me closer, near.
And though the world may drift away,
In you, I find my brightest day.
For you are more than just a dream,
You are the truth, the quiet beam—
Of light that guides me through the night,
And makes my world forever bright.

Eternal Flame

They say that flames can flicker, die,
But ours, it burns beyond the sky.
A fire that knows no end or start,
It's born within the purest heart.
No wind can make this love grow cold,
No force can break what we both hold.
For in your arms, I feel the heat,
Of love so strong, so pure, so sweet.
It lights the dark, it warms the air,
A love that's bound beyond compare.
And even when the ashes fall,
This flame, it conquers over all.
So let them watch, let them admire,
But only we can hold this fire.
A love that never burns away,
But only grows with every day.

More Than Words Can Say

If I could write a million lines,
They still could never touch the signs—
Of love that runs so wild, so deep,
A love that never falls asleep.
For even words can't quite express,
The way your love, it brings me rest.
No poem, no rhyme, no song could show,
The way my heart will always know.
You are my muse, my every thought,
The love I've lived, the life I've sought.
And though I write with all my might,
I still can't match your perfect light.
For you, my love, are more than words,
A song that only silence stirs.
And in your heart, I find my way,
A love that no words could convey.

Uncharted Territory

Love maps often sketch a line,
But ours defies each boundary, each sign.
In lands untouched by ordinary sight,
We chart a course through pure delight.
No compass can direct our course,
For our love flows with its own force.
It's in the wild, the untamed space,
Where we find our sacred place.
We journey through an unknown land,
With nothing but our hearts and hand.
No path is set, no guide to show,
Just love that only we can know.
So let the world remain unplanned,
We'll carve our way through shifting sand.
For in this love, so rare and true,
We find the place we both pursue.

In Every Sunrise

Each sunrise brings a new day's light,
But none can match our love so bright.
The dawn may paint the skies with hue,
But it can't compare to what we do.
Your touch is warmth beyond the sun,
A fire that burns when day is done.
And though the morning light may claim,
It can't outshine our burning flame.
The day will come, the day will go,
But in your eyes, I find my glow.
So let the sun rise as it may,
For you're my light, my endless day.

In the Stillness

In moments when the world stands still,
I feel your presence, warm and real.
No sound is needed, no word is said,
For love like ours is clearly spread.
It's in the stillness, soft and pure,
That I find a love that's sure.
A gentle breeze, a quiet night,
Your love is my eternal light.
No need for noise, no need for cheer,
Just being close when you are near.
For in the silence, hearts can speak,
A love so strong, it's never weak.
So let the world grow hushed and deep,
I'll cherish this in every sleep.
For in the stillness, you're my peace,
A love that will never cease.

A Dance of Souls

Our love's a dance of grace and might,
A waltz that shines through darkest night.
With every step, with every sway,
We find a rhythm, come what may.
The music plays, both soft and grand,
As we move close, hand in hand.
No steps are forced, no tune is wrong,
We dance to our own timeless song.
In every beat, our hearts align,
A love that's truly so divine.
No partner could ever take your place,
For you complete this sacred space.
So let the world keep dancing on,
Our love's a perfect, endless song.
In every dance, in every move,
Our hearts will find their gentle groove.

The Heart's Eternal Echo

Love's echoes can be faint or loud,
But ours is clear, it's unbowed.
In every beat, in every sound,
It's your name that I have found.
The echoes of our love will ring,
Through every season, every spring.
No force can mute this endless song,
For in your heart, I do belong.
The world may try to cast its shade,
But our love's echoes will not fade.
For in this sound, this endless tone,
We find a love that's truly known.
So let the echoes rise and swell,
In every sound, in every bell.
For in this heart, the song will play,
A love that never goes away.

A Universe for Two

The universe is vast and wide,
But in your love, I take my stride.
No star is distant, no space too great,
When I'm with you, it's all so straight.
Galaxies may swirl and spin,
But in your eyes, I always win.
The cosmos holds no secret vast,
That could outshine our love that lasts.
In every star, in every light,
We find our love, so pure, so bright.
No matter where the heavens turn,
In you, my heart will always burn.
So let the universe expand,
I'll always find you, hand in hand.
For in this space, this starry view,
There's nothing but my love for you.

The Song of Us

Our love is more than just a tune,
It's every note, from night to noon.
It's melodies that rise and fall,
A harmony that conquers all.
The song we sing is soft and grand,
A rhythm only we understand.
No words can quite express the feel,
Of love that's perfectly real.
In every verse, in every rhyme,
We find a love that stands the time.
And though the world may play its song,
Ours is the one where we belong.
So let the music play and sway,
For in your heart, I find my way.
The song of us will never cease,
A love that brings eternal peace.

The Unseen Magic

Magic's often seen, not felt,
But in our love, it's deeply dwelt.
It's not in spells or charms we cast,
But in the way our hearts are fast.
The magic here is pure and true,
A force that only binds us two.
No wand could bring what you provide,
No spell could match this love inside.
It's in the quiet, in the calm,
A gentle touch, a soothing balm.
And though it's subtle, soft, and kind,
It's a magic that's uniquely mine.
So let the world search high and low,
For we've found magic in our flow.
In every glance, in every touch,
Our love's the magic that's enough.

In the Embrace of Time

Time may pass and seasons change,
But our love stays within the range.
It stretches wide, it holds so tight,
An embrace that feels so right.
No matter how the years may roll,
This love will always be my goal.
For in your arms, I find my place,
A timeless love, a warm embrace.
The clock may tick, the world may spin,
But in your heart, I'm sure to win.
For time can't touch what's truly ours,
A love that blooms like endless flowers.
So let the hours drift away,
Our love remains, come what may.
In every second, every chime,
I'll cherish you through all of time.

A Love Beyond the Stars

Stars may twinkle in the night,
But none can match our love's pure light.
It shines beyond the cosmic veil,
A love that's destined not to fail.
In every star, in every glow,
Our love is seen, it's deeply known.
No constellation could portray,
The way our hearts connect each day.
So let the galaxies unfold,
Our love's a story yet untold.
And in the stardust, we will find,
A love that's truly one of a kind.
For even stars can't hold the sway,
Of love that grows with every day.
So as the cosmos keeps its chart,
I'll love you with a boundless heart.

A Love So Rare

In a world of fleeting moments and chance,
We found a love that made us dance.
So rare, so true, a precious find,
A love that binds the heart and mind.
It's not in words or grand display,
But in the simple, everyday.
A glance, a touch, a knowing smile,
That makes our love worthwhile.
No one could ever quite explain,
The depth of what we both attain.
For in this love, so rich and rare,
We find a bond beyond compare.
So let them seek what they may seek,
Our love's the treasure that's unique.
And in its rarity, we stand,
With hearts entwined, hand in hand.

Through Every Storm

Storms may rage and winds may howl,
But in your arms, I feel no foul.
A love that stands through every gale,
A beacon bright, a guiding sail.
Though thunder cracks and lightning strikes,
Our love remains through all the hikes.
It's in the calm after the storm,
A shelter warm, a love reborn.
The world outside may tremble, quake,
But in your arms, I find my stake.
A love so strong it will not break,
No storm can cause our hearts to shake.
So let the weather play its part,
Our love's a fortress, a work of art.
And through each tempest, loud and wild,
We'll face it together, reconciled.

A Love Like No Other

Many claim their love's the best,
But ours surpasses all the rest.
A love that's rare, a love that's true,
A love that only we can view.
No tales or songs could quite relay,
The way our hearts find their way.
For in our love, so pure and new,
We've found a bond that's rare and true.
It's not in gifts or grand acclaim,
But in the quiet, gentle flame.
A love that's unique, a love that's bright,
A love that feels so perfectly right.
So let them boast, let them declare,
For we've found a love beyond compare.
And in this truth, we find our own,
A love like no other ever known.

A Love's Evolution

We started simple, hearts untrained,
And through the years, our love has gained.
An evolution, soft and grand,
A journey we took hand in hand.
No map could guide, no plan could chart,
The way our love grew from the start.
It's in the changes, the gentle shift,
A love that's always sure to lift.
From every trial, from every test,
We've found our love can't be suppressed.
It's ever-growing, ever new,
A love that's deep, sincere, and true.
So let's embrace this evolution,
A love that's marked by pure devotion.
For in our hearts, the change is clear,
A love that grows with each new year.

The Magic of Now

In this moment, here and now,
I find a love that shows me how
To cherish every single beat,
To make each second feel complete.
It's in the present, pure and bright,
Where love reveals its greatest light.
No past regrets, no future fear,
Just the magic of having you near.
So let the world fade out of view,
For in this moment, it's just us two.
And in the now, our hearts align,
A love so perfect, so divine.
For in the present, we find grace,
A love that time cannot erase.
And in each breath, in every sigh,
We find the magic of our sky.

In the Warmth of Your Embrace

Your embrace is more than just a hold,
It's a comfort, soft and bold.
A place where worries gently fade,
A haven from the world's cascade.
In your arms, I find my rest,
A shelter that's forever blessed.
No other touch can quite compare,
To the warmth and love you share.
The world may spin, the seasons change,
But in your hold, nothing feels strange.
For there's a peace that I've embraced,
In every moment, love is traced.
So hold me close, and never part,
For in your arms, I find my heart.
A love that's true, a love so clear,
A warmth that's always near.

The Symphony of Us

Our love's a symphony, a grand design,
A melody that's so divine.
Each note, each chord, each perfect sound,
Plays a tune that knows no bound.
In harmony, we find our place,
With every beat, with every grace.
No song could ever match the score,
Of love that we both adore.
So let the music play its role,
Our love's the rhythm of the soul.
And as we dance to this sweet song,
We know that we, together, belong.
For in the symphony we make,
Our hearts will never need to fake.
It's a love that's perfectly composed,
In every note, it's brightly posed.

An Eternal Gift

Your love is a gift, so rare and sweet,
A treasure that no one could ever beat.
It's not in gold or silver bright,
But in the way you hold me tight.
A gift that grows with every day,
A love that never fades away.
No wrapping needed, no grand reveal,
Just the way your heart makes me feel.
So cherish this, the gift we've found,
A love that's deep, that knows no bound.
For in your heart, I see the light,
Of a gift that's perfect, pure, and right.
And though the world may shift and change,
Our love remains, it won't estrange.
An eternal gift that we both share,
A bond that's truly rare and fair.

A Love Beyond Compare

They say that love is everywhere,
But ours is special, beyond compare.
It's not in flowers or fleeting charms,
But in the way you hold me in your arms.
No other love could ever find,
The place that you've carved in my mind.
It's in the moments, big and small,
Where we find our love through it all.
So let them search for love they seek,
For ours is strong, it's never weak.
A love that's built on trust and care,
A love that's truly beyond compare.
And in each day, in every view,
I'll always cherish you, it's true.
For in your heart, I've found my place,
A love that's filled with endless grace.

An Endless Journey

Our love is a journey, never done,
A path we walk with the rising sun.
With every step, with every mile,
We find new reasons to smile.
No destination to define,
Just a journey where hearts align.
Through every twist, through every turn,
A love that always will return.
So let the road be long and wide,
With you, my love, I'll always ride.
For in this journey, we'll find our way,
A love that grows with each new day.
And as we travel, hand in hand,
We'll cherish every grain of sand.
For in this endless road we see,
A love that's meant for you and me.

A Love Beyond Time

In moments where the seconds pause,
I find a love that breaks all laws.
Not bound by hours or days that pass,
But a timeless love that will forever last.
Our hearts beat in a rhythm so true,
In every glance, I find you.
No clock can measure what we feel,
A love that's profoundly real.
As days turn into nights so deep,
Our love is a promise we'll always keep.
For in the fabric of time we weave,
It's your heart that I truly believe.

The Warmth of Your Soul

When the world grows cold and gray,
Your love brings warmth, a lighted ray.
It's not in grand gestures or bright displays,
But in the simple, quiet ways.
Your smile, a beacon in the night,
Your touch, a gentle, warming light.
In every moment, I find my place,
In the warmth of your tender embrace.
So when the storms begin to roar,
I'll seek the warmth of your soul once more.
For in your love, I find my sun,
A light that shines when day is done.

The Heart's True Compass

In a world where directions may stray,
Your love is my compass, guiding the way.
It points to where my heart should be,
In the path that's meant for you and me.
No map or chart could ever show,
The love that in our hearts does grow.
It's in the moments, quiet and clear,
That I find my way when you are near.
So let the world shift and turn,
Our love's the compass we both yearn.
For in your heart, I find my guide,
A love that will forever abide.

The Essence of Us

Our love's not a fleeting fire,
But an essence that will never tire.
It's in the breath we share, the unspoken bond,
A love that's deep and far beyond.
In every whisper, in every sigh,
We find the truth that will never lie.
It's the quiet moments, the tender touch,
The essence of us means so much.
So let the world's noise fade away,
For in our love, we choose to stay.
In the essence of what we are,
We find a love that's our guiding star.

In the Quiet of Our Hearts

In the quiet of our hearts, we find,
A love so gentle, so intertwined.
No words are needed, no grand affair,
Just the comfort of knowing you're there.
It's in the silence where we speak,
In the moments that are soft and meek.
A love that's felt without a sound,
In the quiet, our hearts are found.
So let the world be loud and fast,
In the quiet, our love will last.
For in the stillness of what we share,
We find a love beyond compare.

The Beauty of Our Journey

Every step we take together,
Forms a story that's light as a feather.
It's not in the destination we seek,
But in the journey, so unique.
With every turn and every mile,
We find new reasons to smile.
The beauty lies in the path we tread,
In the love that's always spread.
So let the journey continue on,
With you, my love, I've always won.
For in each moment, big or small,
Our journey's the greatest gift of all.

In Every Breath

In every breath, I find you near,
A love that's strong, a love sincere.
It's not in grand declarations made,
But in the quiet breaths we've laid.
With every inhale, with every sigh,
I feel our love reach the sky.
In the simple act of breathing deep,
Our love is a promise we keep.
So in each breath, in each moment shared,
I find a love that's truly rare.
For in the rhythm of our lives,
Our love forever thrives.

A Love Written in Stars

Our love's a story written in stars,
A tale of hearts that's never far.
It's not in constellations or celestial lore,
But in the way our hearts adore.
The night sky holds our secret script,
A love that's deep and never eclipsed.
In every star, in every light,
Our love shines through the darkest night.
So let the universe unfold its play,
For our love will light the way.
In the cosmic dance of what we share,
We find a love beyond compare.

The Echo of Us

Our love's an echo that never fades,
A sound that's felt in the quiet glades.
It's not in the noise or the bustling crowd,
But in the gentle whispers we've avowed.
In every echo, in every call,
We find a love that stands tall.
It's in the softest, faintest sound,
That our love's true essence is found.
So let the world make all its noise,
In the echo of us, we find our joys.
For in the silent, tender tone,
Our love's the greatest ever known.

The Language of Your Eyes

In the silence of your gaze,
I read a love that truly stays.
No words are needed, no voice can tell,
The stories your eyes reveal so well.
Each glance, a verse, a whispered song,
In your eyes, I feel I belong.
The language of your eyes, so clear,
Speaks a love that's always near.
No book or poem could quite describe,
The way your eyes make my heart vibe.
In their depth, I find my place,
A love that time cannot erase.

Beneath the Surface

Beneath the surface, deep and still,
Our love flows, a gentle thrill.
It's not in the surface, bright and grand,
But in the depths where we both stand.
In quiet moments, in hidden depths,
We find our love's true steps.
It's in the places not often seen,
That our love's essence lies serene.
So let the world see what it may,
For beneath the surface, we'll stay.
In the depth of what we share,
Our love's a treasure beyond compare.

The Warmth of Your Touch

The warmth of your touch, a soothing balm,
A peace that brings a quiet calm.
It's not in grand gestures or loud displays,
But in the subtle, tender ways.
Your touch, a promise, soft and true,
A reminder that I'm close to you.
In every caress, in every embrace,
I find a love I can't replace.
So let the world rush on its path,
In your touch, I find my hearth.
For in the warmth you always give,
Our love's the reason that I live.

A Love's Gentle Strength

Our love's a strength, so soft, so kind,
A gentle force that's intertwined.
It's not in the loud or fierce displays,
But in the quiet, steadfast ways.
In every challenge, in every test,
Our love remains, it's truly blessed.
It's in the strength that holds us tight,
A love that's true and ever bright.
So let the storms come and go,
Our love's the strength we always know.
In every trial, in every strife,
We find a love that's full of life.

The Light in Your Eyes

In the light that shines from your eyes,
I find a love that never lies.
It's not in the words or grand designs,
But in the way your heart aligns.
The light in your eyes, a beacon clear,
Guides me through each doubt and fear.
In their glow, I find my way,
A love that grows with each new day.
So let the world see what it may,
In your eyes, I find my stay.
For in their light, my heart does rest,
A love that's truly blessed.

The Rhythm of Us

Our love's a rhythm, steady and true,
A dance we share in all we do.
It's not in the steps or grand ballet,
But in the rhythm we find each day.
In every beat, in every sway,
We find our love in a gentle play.
It's in the moments, soft and sweet,
Where our hearts and rhythms meet.
So let the music play its part,
In the rhythm of us, we find our heart.
For in this dance, in every beat,
Our love's the song that's ever sweet.

An Unspoken Bond

In the quiet of our shared space,
I feel an unspoken grace.
It's not in the words or what's been said,
But in the bond that's silently spread.
In every glance, in every sigh,
We share a love that's deep and nigh.
It's in the silent moments we've known,
That our unspoken bond has grown.
So let the world make all its sound,
In our silence, our love is found.
For in the quiet, tender and true,
I find an endless love in you.

The Embrace of Night

As night descends and shadows play,
I find your love in a soft array.
It's not in the day's bright, glaring light,
But in the embrace of the gentle night.
In every star, in every moonbeam,
Our love's a calm, unspoken dream.
It's in the quiet of the evening's hue,
That I feel most close to you.
So let the night unfold its grace,
In your embrace, I find my place.
For in the darkness, soft and deep,
Our love's the promise we always keep.

A Love That Transcends

Our love transcends the bounds of time,
A connection so pure, so sublime.
It's not in the moments fleeting fast,
But in the eternity that we've cast.
In every heartbeat, in every sigh,
We reach for the stars in the sky.
It's a love that knows no end,
A bond that's meant to always mend.
So let the world's limits fall away,
Our love transcends each passing day.
For in the eternity we've designed,
Our hearts and souls are forever aligned.

In the Quiet Moments

In the quiet moments we both share,
I find a love beyond compare.
It's not in the loud or the grand display,
But in the silence where we find our way.
In every soft touch, in every glance,
We build a love that's our own dance.
It's in the subtle, gentle grace,
That I find my favorite place.
So let the world rush and roar,
In our quiet moments, I adore.
For in the stillness, pure and true,
I find a love that's meant for me and you.

A Little Note :)

Though we may be miles apart, my thoughts are with you every single day. Even from a distance, your presence is a constant in my mind, and I cherish you in every moment :)

About the Author

Mrigendra Bharti, born on June 29, 2004, in South Delhi, India, is a multifaceted individual recognized as the owner of Mrigendra Bharti Group InfoTech India Co. Pvt Ltd. Beyond his entrepreneurial endeavors, he is a distinguished music producer, director, and a budding writer.

Embarking on his professional journey at a young age, Mrigendra Bharti's visionary leadership has led to the establishment of several successful ventures, including Croma Music Series Entertainment, Sellbrochure, Fauget Innovative, and more.

What sets Mrigendra apart is his early initiation into the world of business. His foray into the unknown realms of entrepreneurship began during his 10th-grade years, where he delved into the music industry. This initial venture laid the foundation for subsequent achievements, showcasing his dedication and resilience.

Having honed his skills in music, Mrigendra Bharti not only demonstrated significant growth in his craft but also expanded his professional network. His passion extends beyond music, encompassing app and website development, as well as graphic design.

Fueled by his creative aspirations, Mrigendra established the Mrigendra Bharti Group, a company specializing in website and app development. Currently, he collaborates with a dedicated team, collectively working on ambitious projects that promise innovation and excellence.

Mrigendra's journey serves as an inspiration, particularly for today's students, highlighting the potential of youthful determination and the ability to transform innovative ideas into successful businesses. As he continues to make strides in various domains, Mrigendra Bharti remains a dynamic force, contributing vibrancy to the realms of business, music, and technology.

Read more at https://www.imwriter-mrigendra.rf.gd.

9 798822 719233